AF377657

WORLD WAR I: PART TWO

1915-1917: Stalemate

Written by Benjamin Janssens de Bisthoven
Translated by Rebecca Neal

WORLD WAR I, 1915-1917: STALEMATE

KEY INFORMATION

- **When:** 28 July 1914 – 11 November 1918.
- **Where:** Europe, Asia, Africa and Oceania.
- **Countries involved:**
  - The Central Powers: Germany, Austria-Hungary, Bulgaria, the Ottoman Empire.
  - The Allies and associated countries: the British Empire, France, Tsarist Russia, Italy, Serbia, the USA, Japan, China, Belgium, Romania, Portugal, Luxembourg, Greece, Albania, Montenegro and most of the South American countries.
- **Outcome:**
  - Allied victory.
  - Collapse of the German, Austro-Hungarian, Ottoman and Russian Empires.
  - Establishment of new states.
- **Victims:** More than 9 million dead.

INTRODUCTION

In the winter of 1915, Europe was in a bloody stalemate. Since the assassination of Archduke Franz Ferdinand (1863-1914) turned into an insurmountable international crisis in July 1914, war had been raging between Austria-Hungary and its ally Germany, and the Triple Entente, a coalition between France, Britain and Russia, which had been joined by Belgium and Serbia. This conflict, which everyone had expected to be over quickly, had by this point taken an unexpected turn.

During the autumn of 1914, the plans drawn up by the two camps to secure the victory had collapsed without any decisive result being obtained. On all fronts, the armies, exhausted and drained of their resources, had stopped advancing. In the West, in France and Belgium, millions of men were sheltering in trenches, and the existing means and military tactics proved incapable of driving them out.

The scale of the war surpassed all expectations. It was bloodier than ever before and had already caused a complete massacre: 300 000 French soldiers, 400 000 Russian soldiers and 260 000 German soldiers were dead. The destruction was immense and there were countless refugees. Even the economies of the warring countries were faltering under the weight of an unprecedented mobilisation of men and material. In spite of this, no peace was in sight. On the contrary, the war was beginning again with renewed energy and violence. It spread to new battlefields and new domains, demanding ever-greater involvement from civilians and societies. The conflict was gradually turning into total war.

THE SEARCH FOR A BREAKTHROUGH

Until 1917, Berlin, Vienna, Petrograd (modern-day St Petersburg), Paris and London were driven by the same obsession. They all wanted to upset, in their own favour, the balance established in 1914 by the Battle of Tannenberg and the Battle of the Marne. This would lead to victory. It was a necessary, indispensable step. Otherwise, how was it possible to justify the terrible sacrifices they had already accepted? The countries therefore had to forge ahead. As the means deployed in 1914 had been insufficient, the two sides raised the stakes and extended the war to the spheres of economy, science and diplomacy. Gradually, all of society was involved in the war.

THE EXPANSION OF THE CONFLICT

When hostilities first broke out in August 1914, the war already had a global dimension. The United Kingdom was the world's foremost colonial power, ruling over more than 11 million square miles and 348 million people, from India to Egypt and including Australia, Malaysia, South Africa, New Zealand and Canada. France, meanwhile, had carved itself out a vast empire over the course of the previous century, covering West Africa, Madagascar, Indochina, and Polynesia and New Caledonia in the Pacific. Germany was present in the Solomon, Marshall and Caroline Islands, New Guinea, Togo, Cameroon and Namibia, and had a large colony in East Africa, in the area that would become Tanzania, Rwanda and Burundi. Following the example of the European countries, these territories rose up in turn and made their mark on the course of events until the end of the war.

The longer the war went on, the further it spread. Between 1914 and 1917, numerous participants joined one of the two sides. The stalemate on the main fronts in the winter of 1915 also strongly encouraged the warring nations to ally themselves with new countries and find other battlefields. In addition, the confrontation moved into the world of officialdom, where diplomats and foreign ministers competed to find ever more ingenious ways to win the support of neutral countries.

On the side of the Triple Entente, Japan was the first country to enter the fray. It had been an ally of the United Kingdom since 1902 and went to war against Germany in August 1914, but did not directly take action in Europe. It was followed in May 1915 by Italy, which had received lavish promises from the Triple Entente (transfer of all the Italian-speaking territories of Austria-Hungary, annexation of the Dalmatian Coast, new African colonies, etc.). Then came Portugal in March 1916, after Germany declared war on the country for giving in to pressure from Britain and seizing all the German boats sheltering in its ports. Romania joined in August 1916, inspired by the Russian successes against Austria-Hungary and hoping to get hold of Austro-Hungarian Transylvania, which had a sizeable Romanian minority. The USA joined in April 1917 and Greece joined in July 1917, following a coup incited by the Triple Entente. Moreover, throughout 1917, considerable pressure from the United States would push China and the majority of the countries of Latin America to enter the war against Germany. Nonetheless, these countries would only play a minor role in the conflict.

Germany and Austria-Hungary were less fortunate. Since 1914, they had constantly caused international outrage: the violation of Belgian neutrality, the massacre of civilians in Belgium, France and the Balkans, the gassing of French and British soldiers in April 1915, attacks on enemy and neutral merchant ships, and more. Only two countries joined their cause: the Ottoman Empire in October 1914, which was pushed into war by its growing dependence on Germany and desire to slow its own decline; and Bulgaria in September 1915, as Berlin and Vienna promised the return of territories lost during the Second Balkan War (such as Serbian Macedonia and Greek Thrace).

The globalisation of the war

Although it brought new human and material resources for the Triple Entente and the Central Powers, the expansion of the conflict also increased the number of fronts. While war was already raging in the German colonies, which had been invaded from all sides starting in August 1914, men were also fighting in the Caucasus, the Middle East, Northern Italy and throughout the entire Balkans region. Although these new battlegrounds were only of secondary significance, they played a considerable role both in the continuation of the stalemate and the way out of it. As such, the two sides banked on them to divert enemy troops and material away from the main battlefields. From 1916, both the Triple Entente and the Central Powers fully incorporated them into their strategies to win the war. In 1918, they would even prove decisive: it is on these secondary fronts that Germany was dealt the death blow.

MILITARY ESCALATION

In 1915, the stalemate on the main fronts and the scale of human loss did not at all discourage the two sides from seeking victory through armed conflict. Both the Triple Entente and the Central Powers still thought that they could secure a quick military triumph. To achieve this objective, a series of incredibly ambitious plans were drawn up, while ever-increasing numbers of men and quantities of material were sacrificed. However, these plans did not have the hoped-for results.

After its strategic failure on the Western Front in 1914 – where it had planned to defeat France before turning back towards Russia – the German army decided to reverse its priorities for 1915. Two reasons drove Erich von Falkenhayn (1861-1922), Chief of the German General Staff, to focus on the Eastern Front:

- the weakness of Austria-Hungary, which had been hit hard by the previous year's fighting;
- the intense pressure that was being put on him by the two commanders-in-chief on the Eastern Front, Paul von Hindenberg (1847-1934) and Erich Ludendorff (1865-1937).

Consequently, enemy fire rained down over the Russian army until autumn 1915. Some of these attacks were extremely violent: in May, the Austro-Hungarian and German armies organised bombing on a scale previously unknown in the East, with 1200 cannons, between Gorlice and Tarnów. The overall results of the campaign were impressive: the majority of Poland was occupied, Austro-Hungarian territory which had been invaded in 1914 was liberated, and the Russian army lost over two million men. In the wake of this success, the Central Powers, supported by Bulgaria, crushed Serbia. However, the most important victory was not accomplished, as Russia recovered at the end of the year.

The disjointed Allied attempts were much less successful. In France, French and British troops pounded the German trenches at various points along the front, as much to relieve pressure on the Russians as to force a decisive breach in the enemy line. Neither of these objectives was attained, even when, following its entry into the war in May, Italy launched its own attacks against Austria-Hungary. On both the French and Italian fronts, only a few miles of territory were conquered, and losses were heavy. The British and French landing in the Dardanelles was equally disastrous. This campaign, which aimed to reopen the straits closed by the Ottomans and thus permit the transport of supplies to Russia via the Black Sea, to strike a fatal blow to the Sublime Porte (Istanbul), and to rally the Balkan states which were still neutral, was blocked by the Turkish resistance from the beginning. For the Triple Entente, everything would have to be put off until the following year.

With their armies stuck in a rut in Russia, the Central Powers returned to the Western Front in 1916. Von Falkenhayn wanted to push France, which he thought had been worn out by its failures in 1915, to ask for peace. With this aim in mind, he devised a large-scale action which intended not to decimate the French army, but to show it that it could not hope for any more military success against Germany. His main idea was simple: take control of a key sector held by the French and repel all their counter-attacks to recover it. This sector was Verdun. Vast resources were allocated for the operations. On 21 February, 1200 cannons fired two million shells along a stretch of just ten miles. The impact of the shock was felt as far away as the Vosges. In spite of everything, the badly-designed plan quickly descended into improvisation, and the battle turned into pure attrition. In July, when the fighting was coming to an end, the French were still standing. This was another failure for Germany. Its ally Austria-Hungary was not faring any better. In spite of a strong start, its offensive against the Italians had also turned to stalemate and the erosion of the enemy territory.

| Photograph of French soldiers on the battle-field at Verdun.

Drawing lessons from the previous year, the Allies were somewhat more fortunate this time. They had met at Chantilly in December 1915 and come to an agreement to synchronise their offensives, so as to stop the Germans sending their reserves from one hot spot to another. On 4 June, the Russians got the ball rolling. With the Germans and Austro-Hungarians still occupied at Verdun and in Italy, the tsarist army easily overcame their defences in the East. In one month, it gained around 75 miles on its enemies and took 400 000 Austro-Hungarian prisoners. Unfortunately for the Russians, this great success was jeopardised by the disappointments faced by the Triple Entente in the West. At the start of July, in spite of the tremendous resources used (2700 cannons and three million shells) and a week-long bombardment, the Franco-British attempt to secure a breakthrough on the Somme failed and declined into a war of attrition. The same happened with the attack launched by the Italians in August against the Austro-Hungarians. These misfortunes allowed the Central Powers to regroup in the East. By autumn, the Russians had been badly beaten and were forced to abandon all the territory they had conquered. Once again, the military outcome of the war was put off until the following year.

However, there would be no further escalation in 1917. Exhausted and weary, the two camps no longer had the means or the desire to raise the stakes. Although they were less extravagant, their initiatives would nonetheless still prove to be the turning point in the war.

MOBILISATION AT HOME

The outcome of the Great War depended as much on those behind the lines as on the men at the front. The ambitious military operations and prolonged upkeep of millions of men in the armies demanded economies that were capable of producing and transporting large quantities of supplies, equipment and military material. The warring countries felt this need from the first months of the war. In 1914, they were all without exception affected by shortages and supply difficulties. The problem was the same everywhere: military needs, which far outstripped all predictions before the war, were greater than the immediate economic capacity of the nations. It was therefore essential to increase outputs, especially as demand skyrocketed with the military escalation.

In order to achieve this goal, governments became increasingly involved in the economy, gradually extending their control over raw materials, industries and transport companies. In these strategic domains, state management and coordination organisations were set up, such as the KRA (*Kriegsrohstoffabteilung*, War Raw Materials Department) in Germany and the Wheat Committee in Britain to supply provisions to the Allies. Also illustrative of this trend is the creation of ministries for munitions in Britain and France in 1915. From now on, military interests took priority over everything else. In the countries at war, many factories were forced to convert their production, often to make shells and munitions. New workshops and arsenals were set up in many locations, some at great cost, such as the arsenal at Roanne in central France.

To fuel this vast production effort, workers were indispensable and valuable, as many men were at the front. Moreover, at the start of the war most of the warring countries had made the mistake of mobilising the majority of their workforce. When the first shortages were felt, many workers were summoned back to the factories. In France, over 490 000 men came back behind the lines in 1918, and almost 440 000 did the same in Italy. Eventually, the conscription of specialised workers was forbidden. However, calling back these workers was still not enough to meet the needs of the war. Women were therefore called on to fill in the gaps. According to Jean-Paul Bled, in Austria-Hungary they occupied 25% of positions in the armaments industry. By the end of the war, there were 430 000 women working in French industries and 750 000 working in British industries. France and the United Kingdom also drew on a workforce from their colonies. While they sent hundreds of thousands of soldiers from their colonies to the front, tens of thousands of natives also worked in factories in the cities. Meanwhile, Germany and Austria-Hungary exploited the populations of the territories they occupied. From 1916 onwards, Germany even organised the mass deportation of workers from the conquered countries to the Reich. There were also prisoners of war, who were very widely exploited by both sides, both at the front and behind the lines, often to carry out the most dangerous tasks.

| Women working in a shell factory in France.

As well as increasing the workforce, the governments also worked on production rates. Working days were lengthened in all countries. In Austria-Hungary, a 70-hour workweek was standard, and could even reach 110 hours in the Skoda armament industries. In many factories, teams of workers took shifts day and night. As a whole, discipline behind the lines was tightened and became militarised, even in Western democracies: in the United Kingdom, strikes were outlawed in 1915, and employees were no longer allowed to change jobs.

The war effort required substantial resources. As was the case with the workforce, London and Paris drew on their colonies, while Berlin and Vienna took from the occupied territories. Russia could use its vast empire. Both sides also tried to obtain the resources they needed from neutral countries. The United States and Latin America were in particular courted by the Triple Entente, while the Central Powers had to limit themselves to European countries. The reason for this was simple: here, as on the battlefield, the situation was escalating. Both camps worked to stifle their enemies' economies by stopping their sources of provisions. The Triple Entente, which had control of the sea, held the advantage. A blockade of the Central Powers had been put in place in 1914 and was strengthened throughout the war, and was even eventually applied to the neutral countries bordering Germany and its allies. From 1915, the Germans responded with their submarines, the U-boats. However, this response was clumsy. The *Lusitania* and the *Arabic*, two British liners carrying American passengers, were sunk. The USA threatened Berlin, and Vienna withdrew. The U-boats were then called back. In 1916, during the Battle of Jutland, the Germans tried once again to break the blockade, this time with their fleet of warships. However, this attempt was in vain. By the end of 1916, there were major shortages. People ate bread substitutes made of barley, corn and potatoes. Food and coal were strictly rationed. Requisitions escalated: the Germans and Austro-Hungarians took church clocks, door handles and crockery for metal, mattresses for wool, etc.

| Sinking of the *Lusitania*. Illustration by Norman Wilkinson for *The Illustrated London News*.

The Triple Entente also encountered difficulties. The immense war effort put all the countries to the test. It could not be maintained indefinitely. For example, between 1917 and 1919, France alone was spending an average of 32.4 million dollars per day. At such a pace, the countries' economies would end up collapsing sooner or later.

TECHNOLOGICAL INNOVATION TO THE RESCUE OF THE WAR

As the historian Frédéric Guelton points out, immediately prior to the war all the armies were below their real technical capacity. Convinced that the conflict would follow the model of the Napoleonic Wars, with infantry and cavalry predominating, the general staff disparaged the technological innovations available in favour of more traditional equipment and weaponry, especially because these new technologies risked completely overturning established military doctrines. Consequently, recent inventions such as aeroplanes, submarines and lorries were often relegated to a secondary position in the European arsenals. Meanwhile, innovations under development, such as tanks, did not encounter favourable conditions to be really implemented.

However, the war turned everything upside down. As soon as hostilities broke out, the armies found themselves facing a series of hitherto unseen and unexpected situations, which forced them to reconsider existing dogma and stimulated scientific and technical innovation. The radical transformation of the infantry provides an illustration of this. Uniforms were modernised in response to the horrific losses in the early battles. Conspicuous shades, like the red trousers that the French soldiers were still forced to wear in 1914, were replaced by colours that were more difficult to spot. Modernised reappropriations of medieval armour were incorporated into uniforms as protection: the soldiers' bodies were covered by helmets, body armour and even shields.

The shortage of troops was also accompanied by a spectacular increase in firepower: the use of machine guns became widespread and the light machine gun emerged. Trench warfare also had an impact on weapons. The first flamethrowers were used by the Germans in February 1915 with the aim of destroying bunkers and fortifications more easily. Indirect weapons were also a resounding success. The grenade, which had been invented in the 15th century, became popularised and considerable technical progress was made on it until the end of the war. The same went for grenade launchers and other mortars. Finally, there were also sniper rifles, trench shovels and yataghans (swords with a curved, single-edged blade). The artillery and the cavalry underwent similar changes at the same time.

This ordeal also forced the armies to incorporate existing inventions that had had a bad press until that point, and which now drastically altered warfare. Aviation made a dazzling breakthrough during the first two months of the conflict, superseding the cavalry and being used for detailed reconnaissance. Continual progress was made in this domain. In autumn 1914, the first planes armed with machine guns appeared in the sky, a precursor to modern aerial warfare. With the stalemate on the ground, the bomber, developed before the war, became practically indispensable for striking the uncatchable rearguard of the enemy. By 1918, the warring countries had genuine air fleets which were fully integrated into their military strategy. In March of that year, France and Britain had 4000 planes on the Western Front, compared with 1500 for the Germans. Another triumph was that of the submarines. Although they had been neglected before the war by the majority of admiralties, who saw them as undignified and ineffective machines, they soon became indispensable for success. The Germans were won over by their capacities and, in 1917, made them into a strategic weapon with the aim of winning the war.

There was another phenomenon behind this mania for technology: with the military stalemate and the prolonging of the conflict, the warring countries looked to scientific and technological innovation in their search for a decisive advantage over their enemies. Both sides recruited many industrialists and scientists for this purpose. Two famous inventions of the Great War were a direct result of this: poison gas and tanks. The former was probably first used on the battlefields in August 1914, when the French army used tear gas. In autumn, the Germans bombarded Russian positions around Warsaw with hundreds of tear gas shells. However, the major turning point came in 1915, when a lethal gas was used for the first time. On 22 April of that year, 6000 cylinders of chlorine used by the Germans released their deadly contents over the French and British trenches in Ypres. The front was immediately broken, but this was not exploited. Gas continued to be used until the end of the war, by all the armies and in different forms.

Finally, tanks were developed following of a dual observation: the extreme vulnerability of foot soldiers crossing no man's land, and the difficulty faced by the artillery following their advance. These two problems were responsible for many catastrophes. To get around this, the French and the British had the idea of developing an armoured vehicle that could carry an item of artillery and cross terrain that had been ravaged by the fighting. After a lengthy development phase, the first tanks, which were at this stage very basic, were used in September 1916 by the British, then in April 1917 by the French. In spite of their complete lack of reliability, 6500 tanks were used by the Triple Entente between 1916 and 1918, compared with around 20 on the side of the Germans who, wrongly, never believed in this new weapon.

SUBVERSIVE POLITICS: DISSIDENCE AND NATIONAL MINORITIES

The battles of the Great War were not limited to land, air and sea combats. It was also a war of hearts and minds. From 1914 onwards, intellectuals, religious figures, members of the military and politicians were mobilised in all the warring countries to justify and glorify the war to their fellow citizens, maintain the nation's fighting spirit and undermine enemy populations. The many methods of this mental battle were put into place bit by bit, and included propaganda, censorship, restrictions on individual freedoms, truces in internal social and political fights within countries, espionage and counter-espionage, and the support and financing of subversive groups. During the first few months of the war, this psychological dimension remained limited: the populations' support for the war was generally at its highest, and everybody thought that victory would rapidly be obtained through armed conflict.

Once again, the military stalemate changed everything. The failure of the armies made the psychological war an important means of weakening the enemy and facilitating the accomplishment of the national war aims. It was all the more important because the indefinite prolongation of the conflict sapped the morale of populations and consequently created a favourable climate for internal dissent. Until the armistice, both sides worked to fuel this dissent, targeting in particular oppressed ethnic groups and minorities. On the side of the Central Powers, the Germans and Austro-Hungarians stirred up dissidence and nationalism in Finland, Poland and Ukraine, which were dominated by the Russians. They used the same approach with the Jewish diaspora, creating a committee for the liberation of Russian Jews alongside the league of nations oppressed by Russia. The Ottomans did the same in the Caucasus with Muslim populations conquered by the empire of the tsars in the previous century, such as the Azeri and the Chechens. Further west, Germany tried to divide to divide Flemings and Walloons in occupied Belgium, and encouraged supporters of Irish independence against the British. To harm France and Italy, it incited the colonised peoples in North Africa to revolt and, along with the Ottoman Empire, caused the terrible Senussi rebellion in Libya in 1915. Similar attempts were carried out in Afghanistan and Persia. In November 1914, the Central Powers even issued an appeal to Muslims to embark on a holy war, delivered through the Ottoman sultan Mehmed V (1844-1918). Apart from some desertions in the French and British colonial troops, this appeal went practically unanswered.

On the opposite side, the Triple Entente also worked on the Polish, promising them autonomy within Russian territory in 1914, then independence in 1918. However, its action was focused primarily on the multi-ethnic Austro-Hungarian and Ottoman Empires, which were already weakened by national minorities' fight to have their political rights recognised. In the Austro-Hungarian Empire, it roused Czech, Slovakian, Slovenian, Croat and Italian separatists, who participated in a Congress of Oppressed Minorities in Rome in 1918. Starting in 1917, it would go as far as encouraging the creation of 'national' volunteer units to fight the Central Powers: Czech legions in France, Italy and Russia, as well as Yugoslav and Polish fighters. Against the Ottomans, Russia lured Armenian minorities and other Christian peoples in the Caucasus with the promise of independence. In the Middle East, Britain and France made contradictory promises to the Arabs, who were driven to revolt in 1916 by missions led by Lawrence of Arabia (1888-1935) and Édouard Brémond (1868-1948), and to the Jews, with the 1917 Balfour Declaration in favour of the creation of a national Jewish homeland in Palestine.

It is difficult to evaluate the impact of this psychological warfare on the course of the conflict. Although it gave both sides military support and various advantages (rallying to the cause, demoralisation of enemy troops, diversions, etc.), these were limited in most cases. Politically, it often did nothing more than intensify the radicalisation of national minorities brought about by the war. Austria-Hungary was the only real victim of separatism and collapsed in 1918, above all because its minorities were frustrated by the economic difficulties caused by the war and Vienna's inability to reform the empire into a federation. In reality, the most important and longest-lasting effect of the psychological war was undoubtedly the development of mistrust and a feeling of insecurity in the targeted countries. In North Africa, the German attempts to influence the native inhabitants led to a significant degree of suspicion and hostility towards France. In the Ottoman Empire, the Russian policy towards the Armenians helped to make the Turks suspicious of them, even though they mostly remained loyal to the Sublime Porte. The Armenian Genocide, which began in March-April 1915 and claimed between 800 000 and 1.5 million victims, was deeply rooted in this harmful context. This was also the case with the massacre of Christian communities in Syria, the Assyrian people, by the same culprits, and the forced displacement of Greeks and Kurds.

1917: THE TURNING POINT

31 December 1916 was a sombre New Year for the Triple Entente and the Central Powers, who were more mired in the war than ever. The expansion of the conflict had not yet brought any concrete results. Even worse, the great battles in Verdun and the Somme had only ended in carnage. Germany had seen over 800 000 men injured, killed or disappeared there, compared with 571 000 for France and 420 000 for Britain. In Italy and the Balkans, the human cost was no doubt far greater, but there was still a complete deadlock. In all countries, opposition to the war was developing and becoming structured. The war was running out of steam. In 1917, three major events would rekindle it: the United States' entry into the war, the strategic failure of the Triple Entente and the total collapse of Russia.

THE UNITED STATES' ENTRY INTO THE WAR

At the start of 1917, the USA was neutral and had every intention of remaining so. American public opinion was deeply divided on the world war. Although the president, Woodrow Wilson (1856-1924), dreamt of imposing his ideal of peace based on national self-determination, the freedom of the seas and the creation of an international organisation capable of ensuring collective security (the future League of Nations) on the European nations, he did not plan on using force to achieve this. Finally, it must be pointed out that the USA benefitted from the large-scale conflict between the world's main powers, in particular to further its own strategic aims: in 1916 Wilson signed an important law for the expansion of the American navy, with the aim of equalling the Royal Navy, which was at that time the greatest fleet of the world.

Nonetheless, Germany turned this situation on its head. During the first months of 1917, the German land army was put completely on the defensive for the first time. Although it had managed to recover after the Allied assaults of 1916, it had sustained heavy losses in terms of men and material. Additionally, von Hindenburg and Ludendorff, who had replaced von Falkenhayn in August 1916, were stalling for time until the imperial army had the means to restart the conflict in optimal conditions thanks to a massive mobilisation of the economy. In this context, the German navy was entrusted with the strategic initiative for 1917. On 31 January, Ludendorff announced that all-out submarine warfare against the Allies was to be resumed. Two miscalculations were at the root of this decision. Firstly, the German admiralty thought that it would be possible to take the United Kingdom out of the war in under six months by massively attacking its merchant ships. Although the German generals were less convinced, they were nonetheless counting on the Triple Entente's maritime difficulties to relieve pressure on the Western Front, where they were planning a large-scale attack. Finally, the German generals believed that the United States' entry into the war was not inevitable and would not be fatal, because it would come too late to save the Triple Entente.

The start of the submarine campaign in the Mediterranean and the Atlantic was a great success for the Germans. In February, the U-boats sank almost 540 000 tonnes of Allied merchant ships; this figure reached 594 000 in March and almost 860 000 in April. In London, the British admiralty was left helpless. The United States remained neutral in spite of unusually strong diplomatic pressure. The escalation had nonetheless begun. On 3 February, the USA broke off diplomatic relations with Germany. On 26 February, Wilson asked Congress to arm merchant ships. On the same day, a German submarine torpedoed a liner, killing two American civilians. American public opinion gradually leaned towards support for military intervention. An unexpected event would decisively put the country on the road to war.

On 16 January, Arthur Zimmerman (1864-1940), State Secretary for Foreign Affairs of the German Empire, sent a telegram to his ambassador in Mexico, Heinrich von Eckardt (1861-1944), in anticipation of the USA's possible entry into the war. The document contained a financial offer, a treaty of alliance and the recognition of potential Mexican conquests in the United States. Nonetheless, the proposal was rejected by the Mexican government. The story could have stopped there had Zimmerman's telegram not been intercepted by the British intelligence services, who forwarded it to Washington. Its publication on 1 March aroused the general indignation of Americans, the majority of whom were now in favour of the military option. On 2 April, after a further incident in the Atlantic, Wilson solemnly called on Congress to examine the question of American participation in the war. The die had been cast. On 6 April, the United States officially went to war against Germany.

The Central Powers were now facing certain defeat. Thanks to the United States, the Triple Entente had an overwhelming military, economic and human advantage. American strength was already making itself felt: at the end of April, Washington granted the United Kingdom a one-off advance of 250 million dollars, which was a great relief for the British. The future also looked bleak for another reason: by bringing its ships together in powerfully escorted convoys, London had found a way to stop the German submarines, whose results declined. In spite of everything, Germany still had a chance of getting out of the war without sustaining much more damage. It would be a while until a large number of Americans landed in France, because as of April 1917, their army was minuscule. Even better, Germany could count on the strategic mistakes of the Triple Entente and the total collapse of Russia to play its last cards.

THE STRATEGIC FAILURE OF THE TRIPLE ENTENTE

In December 1916, the Allies once again met in Chantilly to make plans for 1917. They chose the same strategy as the previous years: synchronised attacks on all fronts. However, several events caused this strategy to change.

The first of these was the fall from grace of Joseph Joffre (1852-1931), who had been Commander-in-Chief of the French army since 1914. Joffre proved incompetent and was compromised by his repeated failures, so the French government replaced him with Robert Nivelle (1856-1924), who had been accomplished great feats at Verdun. Nivelle made major changes to the plans devised by his predecessor. He decided that the French would no longer strike with the British forces at the Somme, but rather on the Chemin des Dames, in the Aisne department, where they alone would carry out the main advance. Meanwhile, the British would lead a small auxiliary attack in Arras. This was a very ambitious plan for the worn-out French army.

The other disappointment came from the Russians and Italians, neither of whom were capable of attacking as they had promised in Chantilly. At the start of March, Russia, which was worn down by economic, social and political difficulties, was shaken by a first revolution, known as the February Revolution, which toppled tsarism. To popular enthusiasm, a provisional government with liberal and democratic leanings, dominated by the figure of Alexander Kerensky (1881-1970), replaced the authoritarianism of Nicholas II (1868-1918). Although the new regime promised the Triple Entente that it would remain in the war, it could not participate in the Nivelle Offensive, which was planned for spring. The Russian army was completely falling apart, and would need time to restore discipline. Meanwhile, Italy made clear that it would not commit to the plan without knowing what the enemy's plans were on the Western Front and without receiving reinforcements from its allies. France and Britain could therefore only rely on themselves.

In spite of everything, Nivelle pressed on with his attack on the Chemin des Dames, gathering together the last remaining French forces. His resources were immense: 1.2 million men, 5310 cannons, around a hundred tanks and over 500 planes. This fuelled hopes in the country and in the army that proved to be unfounded: Nivelle's attack hit a wall. The Chemin des Dames was one of the areas of the front that the Germans had fortified the most. They had guessed at the French plans and massed their reserves in the area. In the space of two days, the breakthrough was a complete failure. The Second Battle of the Aisne became a bloodbath, with no major progress on either side, until it ended on 9 May. When the great hopes raised by the offensive were dashed, the morale of the French army plummeted. In mid-May, a vast wave of mass disobedience swept through its ranks, with men refusing to leave the trenches to fight the enemy. Some even threatened to march on Paris. This was a serious warning sign. Philippe Pétain (1856-1951), who replaced Nivelle after the defeat, had to regain control of the army. It was still recovering, and did not take any further decisive action until 1918.

For the Central Powers, the French defeat was an excellent result. With Russia in a precarious state, they now had their hands free to counter the Italians and the British, the only countries who presented a real threat. The task was made easier by the fact that Italy and Britain were not synchronised in their actions. From the end of May until September, the Italians launched disjointed attacks on the Isonzo river and in the department of Trentino. They were all halted by Austria-Hungary. On 31 July, to deprive Germany of its submarine bases on the Belgian coast, the

British then struck from Ypres. Fighting continued until November. Once again, the Germans triumphed, with the United Kingdom only gaining a few miles. Finally, in mid-June there was a final burst from Russia, motivated by the desire of Kerensky's government to increase its credibility in order to push the Allies to negotiate for peace. However, it was mercilessly swept away in Galicia by the German and Austrian armies. This was the end of the Triple Entente's strategic offensives.

During the autumn, the initiative passed to Germany and its allies, who would hold on to it until 1918. They quickly scored points against their exhausted enemies. In October, the Italians suffered a humiliating defeat in the Battle of Caporetto. In 11 days, the German and Austro-Hungarian troops advanced 80 miles and captured 300 000 men. The Italian army, which had taken refuge behind the Piave River, was a shadow of its former self. The imperial army resumed its advance against the Russians in September. Within just a few days, they had taken Riga and were directly threatening Petrograd.

RUSSIA LEAVES THE WAR

After the failure of the Kerensky Offensive, Russia entered another turbulent period in June. The morale of the army and the country, which had been low before the attack, dropped to a critical level. There were increasing numbers of desertions, strikes and demonstrations. More than ever, the Russians wanted peace, but the provisional government could not give it to them. It had lost credibility in the eyes of the Allies following the Russian defeat, and it no longer had the strength or the authority to persuade them to sign a general peace with the Central Powers. At the same time, nobody in the government was prepared to sign a separate peace on behalf of Russia.

This was not the only source of dissatisfaction with the ruling powers. The poor economic situation, which had brought down tsarism in March, continued to worsen. Almost completely subservient to the needs of the military, the Russian economy was on its way to completely falling apart. The fact that the majority of vehicles were being used by the army meant that there were not enough to supply the towns and cities, which suffered serious shortages of food and other consumer goods, even though the harvests were comfortably large enough to feed them. Life at the front was hardly any better: the six million soldiers who had been mobilised were poorly fed and badly equipped. Everywhere, inflation climbed while the black market and corruption increased. Above all, the actions, or rather the inaction, of the government disappointed a series of aspirations which had been raised by the February Revolution. First of all were the aspirations of the workers, who had hoped for an improvement in their working and living condi-tions, which were appalling at the time; then there were the aspirations of the poor peasants, who were fighting with the landowning aristo-cracy for the fair distribution of land; and finally, there were the aspirations of non-Russian ethnic groups for political autonomy.

Inevitably, the power of the provisional govern-ment crumbled. In July, there was a rebellion in Petrograd, incited by part of a garrison which refused to be sent to the front. The movement soon extended to the workers, who took up weapons and took to the streets. Their rebellion was brutally put down by troops loyal to the government. In August, Kerensky had to face an attempt by the Commander-in-Chief of the Russian army, Lavr Kornilov (1870-1918) to establish a dictatorship, which he saw as the only way of saving the government from the growing unrest. The prime minister narrowly got out of the situation by bringing all the political forces in the country together against the seditious general. In spite of its best efforts, the provisional government was doomed. Chaos prevailed in the countryside, where peasants, tired of waiting for reforms that never came, had started to share out the land belonging to the aristocracy among themselves. The same thing was happening in the factories, where workers and owners clashed violently to impose their will. To top it all off, Ukraine and Finland, who separatist leanings had been subdued by Petrograd over the summer, were no longer obeying orders.

The radical Marxist revolutionary Bolshevik movement took advantage of this unpleasant situation. Since the February Revolution, the party of Lenin (1870-1924) had been continually campaigning for an immediate return to peace, the collectivisation of land and businesses, and national self-determination. Its following had been growing continuously, and by September was at its highest point. As well as their political programme, the Bolsheviks had another asset: they were the only party that had not been part of the provisional government, and had therefore not been discredited by its failures. Kerensky could do nothing to hold back their rise. On the night of the 7 and 8 November, the Bolshevik movement had become strong enough to seize power in Petrograd. Five months later, at Brest-Litovsk, the new rulers of the Kremlin signed a peace treaty with the Central Powers.

| Signing of the Treaty of Brest-Litovsk.

Germany could now focus on the Western Front. The Russian collapse had freed up around fifty divisions to go to the West, giving the Germans clear numerical superiority over the Allies for the first time since 1914. It still had a chance of defeating the French and British armies, but it needed to act quickly, as the first American troops had already started to land in France. For both the Central Powers and the Allies, 1918 brought a terrible race against the clock.

SUMMARY

1914

Aug.: **Japan enters the war against Germany**

Oct.: **The Ottoman Empire allies itself with Germany and Austria-Hungary**

1915

May: **Italy joins the war on the side of the Triple Entente**

Sept.: **Bulgaria allies itself with Germany and Austria-Hungary**

Dec.: The Allies meet in Chantilly

1916

Feb.-Dec.: **Battle of Verdun**

March: **Portugal enters the war against Germany**

July-Nov.: Battle of the Somme

Aug.: **Romania joins the war on the side of the Triple Entente**

- To get out of the stalemate that had developed in autumn 1914, the warring countries devised an increasing number of responses and strategies, and in doing so extended the war to other domains.

- On the battlefields, the two sides engaged in a military escalation, mobilising an ever-increasing number of men and quantity of materials for their operations and turning to increasingly violent methods. In parallel, the continuation of fighting stimulated the search for a decisive technological advantage over the adversary.

- With increasing military needs, the role of the national economies became decisive for continuing the war. With this in mind, stifling the enemy's economy, through a blockade or the destruction of its merchant ships, became a way of winning the war like any other.

- The deadlock on the main fronts encouraged the warring nations to find new allies and other battlefields, but also to work to undermine the enemy's morale, in particular by inciting national minorities to rebel. The war extended across the world.

- In spite of everything, the strategic impasse persisted. At the start of 1917, both sides were still in a state of equilibrium.

- This equilibrium was disturbed over the course of the year, with the Russian Revolution, the United States' entry into the war on the side of the Allies, and the failure of the Allied offensives. This left Germany in a position of provisional superiority, and the Allies with the assurance that they would win the war in the long term.

We want to hear from you!
Leave a comment on your online library
and share your favourite books on social media!

FIND OUT MORE

BIBLIOGRAPHY

- Barjot, D. ed. (2012) *Deux guerres totales. 1914-1918 1939-1945 : la mobilisation de la nation*. Paris: Economica.

- Defente, D. (2003) *Le Chemin des Dames. 1914-1918*. Paris: Somogy.

- Figes, O. (1997) *A People's Tragedy: The Russian Revolution, 1891-1924*. London: Pimlico.

- Goya, M. (2014) *L'invention de la guerre moderne. Du pantalon rouge au char d'assaut. 1871-1918*. Paris: Tallandier.

- Keegan, J. (2014) *The First World War*. London: The Bodley Head.

- Laparra, J.-C. (2006) *La machine à vaincre : de l'espoir à la désillusion. Histoire de l'armée allemande. 1914-1918*. Quercy: Éditions 14-18.

- Le Naour, J.-Y. (2014) *1916. L'enfer*. Paris: Perrin.

- Mazower, M. (1999) *Dark Continent: Europe's Twentieth Century*. London: Penguin.

- Miquel, P. (1983) *La Grande Guerre*. Paris: Fayard.

- Miquel, P. (1997) *Le Chemin des Dames*. Paris: Éditions de la Seine.

- Offenstadt, N. (2006) *Le Chemin des Dames. De l'événement à la mémoire*. Paris: Perrin.

- Prior, R. and Wilson, T. (2003) *The First World War*. London: Orion Publishing Group.

- Rogan, E. (2015) *The Fall of the Ottomans: The Great War in the Middle East, 1914-1920*. London: Allen Lane.

- Schnetzler, B. (2006) *Les erreurs stratégiques pendant la Première Guerre mondiale*. Paris: Economica.

- Stevenson, D. (2005) *1914-1918: The History of the First World War*. London: Penguin.

- Stevenson, D. (2012) *With Our Backs to the Wall: Victory and Defeat in 1918*. London: Penguin.

- Thompson, M. (2010) *The White War: Life and Death on the Italian Front, 1915-1919*. New York: Basic Books.

- Tooze, A. (2015) *The Deluge: The Great War and the Remaking of Global Order*. London: Penguin.

- Wesseling, H. (2009) *Les empires coloniaux européens. 1915-1919*. Paris: Gallimard.

- Winter, J. ed. (2016) *The Cambridge History of the First World War. Volume II: The State*. Cambridge: Cambridge University Press

ADDITIONAL SOURCES

- Gatrell, P. (2005) *Russia's First World War: A Social and Economic History*. Abingdon: Routledge.

- Horne, A. (1993) *The Price of Glory: Verdun 1916*. London: Penguin.

- Jankowski, P. (2016) *Verdun: The Longest Battle of the Great War*. Oxford: Oxford University Press.

- Levine, J. (2009) *Forgotten Voices of the Somme*. London: Ebury Press.

- Prior, R. and Wilson, T. (2006) *The Somme*. New Haven, Connecticut: Yale University Press.

- Sebag-Montefiore, H. (2016) *Somme: Into the Breach*. London: Penguin.

ICONOGRAPHIC SOURCES

- Photograph of French soldiers on the battlefield at Verdun. Royalty-free reproduction picture.

- Sinking of the *Lusitania*. Illustration by Norman Wilkinson for *The Illustrated London News*. Royalty-free reproduction picture.

- I Want You for US Army. Royalty-free reproduction picture.

- Signing of the Treaty of Brest-Litovsk. Royalty-free reproduction picture.

IMPROVE YOUR GENERAL KNOWLEDGE

IN A BLINK OF AN EYE !

www.50minutes.com

www.50minutes.com

Ebook EAN: 9782806289834

Paperback EAN: 9782806293718

Legal Deposit: D/2017/12603/64

Cover: © Primento

Digital conception by Primento, the digital partner of publishers.